Sk8 for Jake

Written by
Rob Waring and **Maurice Jamall**

Before You Read

to fly		skateboard	
to jump		skate stage	
to skate		ticket	
bench		truck	
phone		excited	
poster		late	
sk8 = sk(eight) = skate		worried	

In the story

John

Eric

Yoko

Mr. Walker

Jake

"Look at me," says John. "I'm flying!" John is jumping with his skateboard. John, Eric, and Yoko are skating in the park. They are good skateboarders.

"Wow, John, that's great," says Eric.

"Watch this," says Yoko. She jumps over the bench with her skateboard.

A man comes to them. He is Mr. Walker and he works in the park. Mr. Walker is angry. "Stop that!" he says. "Do not play on the benches!"

Yoko says, "But we like skating here, Mr. Walker."

Mr. Walker says, "The benches are for people, not for skateboards. No skating here. Go away."

Yoko, John, and Eric are in town. They have their skateboards, but they are not happy. They want to skate in the park. Yoko sees a poster. She runs to it. "Hey!" says Yoko. "Come and look at this!"
Eric and John go over to Yoko.

She shows them the poster. "Wow!" they say. "Look, it's *Jake Montoya and his Skate Stage*!" says John.

Eric says, "They're coming here to Bayview Park. That's great!"

"Wow, Jake Montoya!" says Yoko. "He's the number one skateboarder in the world!"

Eric says, "Let's go. Let's go and buy the tickets today."

It is the big day! Jake Montoya's men and their truck come. The men make the skate stage.
"Look at that," says John. He's looking at the skate stage. "I want to skate on that."
Yoko says, "I want a skate park like this here in Bayview."
"But where's Jake Montoya?" asks John.
Yoko says, "I don't know."

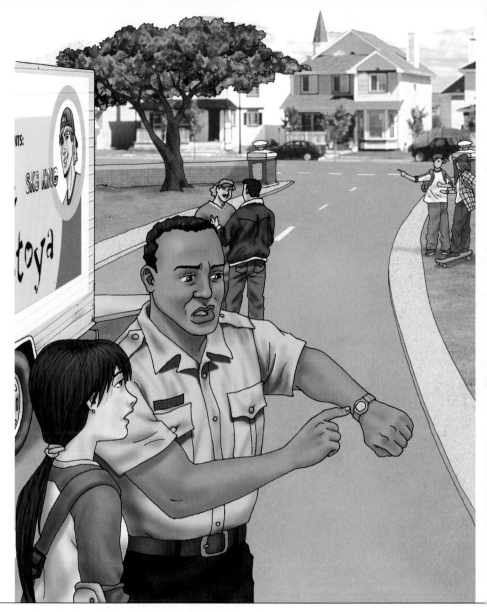

Yoko asks Mr. Walker, "Where's Jake Montoya? Is he here?"
Mr. Walker says, "No. He's late. The show starts at one o'clock."
They look up the street. They do not see Jake.
"Look at the time," says Mr. Walker. "Where is he?"
Mr. Walker is not happy. He is worried. Jake is late.

A man is talking on the phone.
"Oh no!" he says. "Really? Oh, okay. Bye."
"Where's Jake now?" asks his friend.
The man says, "Jake's late. He's coming at two o'clock."
Mr. Walker is listening to the man. Now he is very worried.
Many people have tickets for the show.
"What do I do now?" he thinks.

Yoko and Eric look at the skate stage. It says *Jake Montoya Sk8 Stage*.

"Wow! Look at that," says Yoko. "I like Jake's stage!"

Mr. Walker is listening to them. He knows they are good skateboarders. He has an idea.

Mr. Walker says, "Jake Montoya's late. Do you want to go on Jake Montoya's skate stage?" he asks.

"Oh yes, please," they say. "Yes, please!"

Mr. Walker talks to the man. He tells the man about Eric, Yoko, and John.

Mr. Walker says, "Jake Montoya's late. They want to go on the skate stage. They are very good skateboarders. People can watch them. Is that okay?"

"That's a great idea!" says the man.

Yoko is very excited. "Great! Thanks!" she says.

"Let's go! John, Eric, come on."

They go to the skate stage. They start to skate.
Everybody watches them.
"This is great!" says Yoko.
"Yeah," says Eric. "Really great!"
John says, "Watch this!" He jumps very high.
People buy tickets for the *Jake Montoya Show*.
Many people buy ice cream and hot dogs, too.

Then Jake Montoya comes to the park.

Yoko sees Jake. "Jake Montoya! Wow. Umm. . . Hi, Mr. Montoya."

"Hi. Call me Jake," he says. "Thanks for helping us."

"You're welcome, Jake," says Eric.

Jake says, "You're very good skateboarders!"

"Do you want to skate with me?" asks Jake.

"Yes, please," say Eric and Yoko. They go on the skate stage. Yoko, Eric, and John are very excited. They are skating with Jake Montoya! They have a great time with Jake. He shows them many things. Everybody is very happy.

"Thanks for the show, Jake," says Mr. Walker. "Really great."
"Thanks again, everybody. You're really good skateboarders," says Jake. "Here are some T-shirts for you."
John says, "Wow! Thanks, Jake!"
"I want to say thank you, too," thinks Mr. Walker. He has an idea.

Four weeks later, John, Eric, and Yoko come to Bayview
Park. There is a new skate park.
Eric says, "Wow, look at that!"
"This is for you and your friends," says Mr. Walker to Yoko.
"Thanks, Mr. Walker," says Yoko.
John says, "Let's go, everybody!"
"I want to try, too," says Mr. Walker.

The New Guitar

Written by
Rob Waring and **Maurice Jamall**

Before You Read

to break
(broken)

to clean
something

to drop
something

to fix
something

to jump

band

drums

floor

glue

guitar

keyboard

money

rock star

table

dirty

In the story

Ray   Eric   Mr. Walker

"They are really good," thinks Ray.
He is watching his friends play in their band.
They are playing music at Eric's house.
Eric plays the guitar. Kenji plays the drums, and Yoon-Hee
plays the keyboard.
Ray thinks, "I want to play, too, but I don't have a guitar."

Today it is Ray's birthday. He wants a guitar.
He wants to play the guitar in Eric's band.
He is with his father. His father is looking for a guitar
for Ray's birthday.
They go to the music store. Ray's friend Eric comes, too.
He knows about guitars.

Ray says to his father, "Dad, please buy me this guitar. It's really good!"

Ray's father asks Eric about the guitar.

"Eric, I don't know about guitars. Is this a good guitar, Eric?" he asks.

Eric tells Ray's father about the guitar. "No, it's not a good guitar."

Ray says, "But I want it, Dad. It's great!"

"No, don't buy it, Ray. It's no good," says Eric.

Ray's father says, "Ray, I'm sorry, but I'm not buying it for you."

Ray says, "But . . . Dad. Please!"

"I'm sorry, no," he says. Ray's father buys him a book about guitars.

"Thanks, Dad," Ray says. But he is not happy. He really wants the guitar.

Ray thinks, "I can buy it with *my* money!"

The next day, Ray gets his money from his room.
He goes to the music store. He gives the guitar to the man.
"Can I have this guitar, please?" he says.
Ray buys the guitar. He has no money now, but he is very happy.
He does not tell his mother and father.

Ray goes to Eric's house.
"Eric, look!" says Ray. "I have the guitar now. Do you like it?"
He shows the guitar to Eric.
Eric does not like Ray's guitar. "This isn't a good guitar, Ray,"
says Eric. Ray is not happy, but he wants to play in the band.
Eric looks at Ray. Then he smiles. "Come on, Ray, let's make
some music."

Ray is very happy. Now he can play in the band.
Ray plays the guitar with the band. He is not good, but he likes playing the guitar.
He wants to be a good guitarist.
"This is really great," he thinks. "I love my new guitar!"
The music is not good, but everybody is having a good time.

Ray wants to be a rock star. He likes the band, Dark Sun.
Eric, Kenji, Yoon-Hee, and Ray play many songs.
Ray loves playing his new guitar with the band.
He is not good at playing the guitar, but he is having a
good time. He thinks he is in the band, Dark Sun.

Ray gets very excited. He jumps with his guitar.
But he drops it, and his guitar breaks.
"Oh, no! My guitar! It's broken!" Ray says.
Everybody looks at his guitar. He cannot play music now.
Ray thinks, "What do I do now?"

Ray goes home with his guitar. He wants to fix it.
He wants to play it again. He gets some things to
fix the guitar. He puts them on the table.
He thinks, "I don't want Mom and Dad to see
the broken guitar."

Ray wants to fix the guitar, but he is not very good at fixing things.
"How do I fix it?" he thinks. He looks at his guitar book.
Ray tries to fix the guitar, but he cannot.
"Oh no!" he thinks.

The cat jumps on the table. Some glue goes on the table. "Oh no!" says Ray. The cat walks in the glue. Now glue is everywhere, too.

Ray tries to stop the cat, but he drops the guitar again. It breaks again.

"My guitar!" he says. He is very angry with the cat.

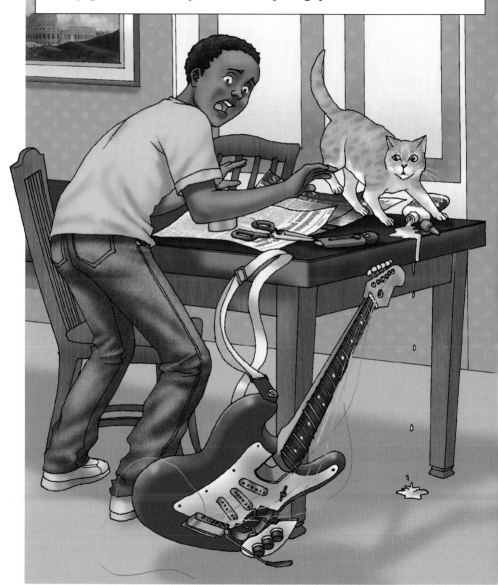

The cat jumps down and walks on the floor. Now the floor is dirty, too.

"Oh, no! The floor!" says Ray.

Ray tries to clean the table. But the table is very dirty.

He tries to clean the floor. But he is not good at cleaning.

Ray's mother and father come home.
"Ray! What's this on the table?" asks his mother.
"And what's this on the floor?"
"What's this guitar doing here?" asks his father.
Ray looks at them and says nothing. He is in
trouble now.

Trouble at the Zoo

Written by
Rob Waring and **Maurice Jamall**

The boys and girls look around the zoo. One of the boys is Mike. He sees a lion.

"Look at that lion!" Mike says to his friend, Scott. Mike goes near the lion's cage.

The lion makes a very loud noise at Mike.

Mike says to the lion, "Hey lion, I'm not scared of you!"

A girl watches Mike. She is very worried. Her name is Jenny.

Trouble at the Zoo

Written by
Rob Waring and **Maurice Jamall**

Before You Read

to close
something

stick

to pick up
something

zoo

to take a
picture

close/
near

bear

dangerous

cage

loud noise

fence

surprised

gate

scared

lion

worried

In the story

Mother
kangaroo

Joey the baby
kangaroo

Mike

Jenny

Mr. Jenkins

"Welcome to Bayview Zoo," says Mr. Jenkins. He works at the zoo.

Today, some students from Bayview High School are at Bayview Zoo.

"Have a good time at the zoo," says Mr. Jenkins.

"But please look at this," he says. He shows them a notice.

The boys and girls look around the zoo. One of the boys is Mike. He sees a lion.

"Look at that lion!" Mike says to his friend, Scott. Mike goes near the lion's cage.

The lion makes a very loud noise at Mike.

Mike says to the lion, "Hey lion, I'm not scared of you!"

A girl watches Mike. She is very worried. Her name is Jenny.

Mr. Jenkins says, "Please do not go near these bears. They are dangerous."
Mike does not listen to Mr. Jenkins. He picks up a stick.
Mike says to his friend, Scott, "Hey, Scott, watch this!"
He hits the cage with the stick. Now the bear is angry, too.

Mr. Jenkins sees Mike and says, "Stop! Don't do that! Bears are
dangerous."
"Sorry, Mr. Jenkins," says Mike. But he is smiling. He is not sorry.
Mike gives a sandwich to the big old bear. "Here you are,
bears," he says.
Mr. Jenkins sees Mike and says, "Stop that! Sandwiches are very
bad for bears. Don't give food to the animals!"
"Sorry," says Mike. But he is not sorry.

"Oh, it's really small," says Jenny's friend, Sarah. She is looking at a baby kangaroo.

The baby kangaroo's name is Joey.

"I want to take a picture with him," she says.

Mr. Jenkins says, "Yes, they're small, but they're very strong. Don't go near them, please."

"Kangaroos are not dangerous," Mike says to Scott. "Look, it's very small."

Mr. Jenkins goes away. Mike goes over the fence. He picks up the baby kangaroo.
"Jenny, do you want a picture with Joey?" asks Mike.
"Stop, Mike, put him down. He doesn't like it," says Jenny.
Jenny goes over the fence to Mike and says,
"Stop it!"

"Put him down, Mike," says Jenny. "Put him down."
Mike says, "It's okay, Jenny. He's okay with me."
But Jenny is angry with Mike. "Give him to me. Now!" she says.
There is a big kangaroo. It is the baby kangaroo's mother.
She looks at Mike.

The kangaroo's mother comes to Mike and Jenny. She does not look happy.

"Look," says Mike. "It's a big kangaroo. Do you want a picture, Jenny?"

Mr. Jenkins sees Jenny and Mike near the kangaroos.

"Jenny! Mike!" he says. "The mother's angry. You have her baby."

The kangaroo comes very close to Mike and Jenny. She is very big. Very, very big.

Mike and Jenny are very worried and scared now.

"I'm scared, Mike. Help me," says Jenny.

Mike is scared too. "Umm . . . Hello, Mrs. Kangaroo," says Mike. "How are you today?" Mike says.

"Umm . . . here, Jenny, you take Joey." He gives the baby kangaroo to Jenny.

The mother kangaroo is very close. She looks down at Mike and Jenny. She is very, very angry.
Mike looks at the mother kangaroo. The mother looks at her baby.
The big kangaroo makes a very loud noise at Mike.
"Let's go! Now! Run, Jenny!" he says.
Mr. Jenkins says, "Stop! No, don't run! Wait there."

Jenny does not run, but Mike runs to the gate. He goes through the gate and closes it.
Jenny is with the very angry kangaroo! She has its baby. And the mother kangaroo wants her baby back!
"Help me, Mr. Jenkins!" she says.

Mr. Jenkins talks to Jenny.

"It's okay, Jenny," says Mr. Jenkins. "You can get out. I can help you."

Jenny says, "I'm scared, Mr. Jenkins. What do I do?"

"Listen to me. Don't run away. Put the baby kangaroo down, Jenny," he says.

Jenny puts the baby kangaroo down. The mother looks at her baby. Then she looks at Jenny.

"Jenny, don't look at the kangaroo," says Mr. Jenkins.
"Now, walk back to me, Jenny." Jenny walks to Mr. Jenkins.
"That's good, Jenny," says Mr. Jenkins. "Don't look at the
mother. Look down, Jenny."
Jenny walks to the gate.
"Good, Jenny," says Mr. Jenkins. "You're very near the gate
now."
He says, "Good. Come out, now, please."

Jenny goes out of the gate. Sarah runs to Jenny. "Are you okay, Jenny?" she asks.

"I'm okay," says Jenny. "Thanks, Mr. Jenkins."

"Good job, Jenny," says Mr. Jenkins.

Mr. Jenkins is very angry with Mike.

"I'm sorry, Mr. Jenkins," says Mike. "I'm sorry, Jenny. I'm really sorry."

Singer Wanted

Written by
Rob Waring and **Maurice Jamall**

Before You Read

to sing a song		keyboard	
to wear		music	
clothes		pop music	
drums		rock band	
guitar		nervous	

In the story

Jenny Faye Tyler John David Daniela Gemma

"Look, it's Faye's band," says Jenny. She is talking to her friend, Daniela.

Daniela says, "Yes, Faye's in the band, Hot Rock."

Faye is their friend. She plays the keyboard for Hot Rock.

Faye's band wants a new singer.

"Look, Jenny," says Daniela. "Hot Rock wants a new singer. I can join the band."

"That's a great idea! You're a really good singer, Daniela," says Jenny.

Daniela says, "I want to sing in Faye's band. I want to be Hot Rock's singer."

Their friend, Gemma comes to them. "What's this?" she asks.
Jenny tells Gemma about the band.
"Good. I want to sing for Hot Rock," says Gemma.
"Do you want to be in the band, Jenny?" Gemma asks.
Jenny smiles. She says, "No, but Daniela does."

Daniela sings a song with the band. But she does not sing well. She is too nervous.
But Jenny likes Daniela's singing. Faye likes her singing, too. "Good job, Daniela!" she says.
"Don't say that," Daniela says. "I'm a really bad singer."
"No, you're not," says Jenny.

Their friend, Gemma comes to them. "What's this?" she asks.
Jenny tells Gemma about the band.
"Good. I want to sing for Hot Rock," says Gemma.
"Do you want to be in the band, Jenny?" Gemma asks.
Jenny smiles. She says, "No, but Daniela does."

It's Saturday. Today Hot Rock is looking for their new singer. John plays the guitar. Tyler plays the bass guitar, and David plays the drums. Faye plays the keyboard.

Jenny asks Daniela, "Are you okay?"

"No, not really," she says. "I'm really excited, but I'm very nervous. I'm not a good singer."

"Don't be nervous," says Jenny. "And don't worry. Everybody likes your singing."

Faye sees Daniela. She says, "Hi, Daniela. Do you want to be in the band?"

"Yes, I do," says Daniela. "But I'm really nervous."

Gemma comes into the room.

"Look, Gemma Walsh is here," Daniela says.

"She's a really good singer. I can't win now."

Daniela sings a song with the band. But she does not sing well. She is too nervous.

But Jenny likes Daniela's singing. Faye likes her singing, too. "Good job, Daniela!" she says.

"Don't say that," Daniela says. "I'm a really bad singer."

"No, you're not," says Jenny.

Gemma sings for the band, too. She sings very well.
Everybody loves her singing. She is a very good singer.
"She's very good!" thinks Jenny.
Daniela knows Gemma is very good, too.

The band talks about Gemma and Daniela.
David, John, and Tyler want Gemma. But Faye wants Daniela.
"I like Daniela's singing," says Faye.
"Yes, but Gemma is very, very good," says Tyler.
They talk for a long time.

Faye says, "We want Gemma to be the new singer!"
"Thank you, Faye. Thank you, everybody," Gemma says.
She is very happy.
"Congratulations, Gemma," says Daniela.
Daniela is very sad. But she is happy for Gemma.

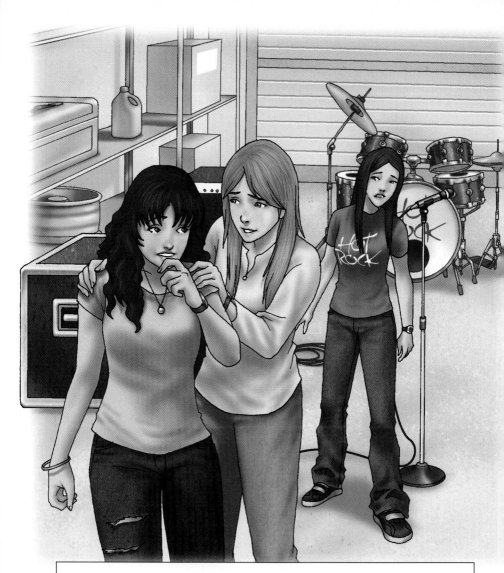

Later, Daniela speaks to Jenny.

"I'm not a good singer. I'm really bad," she says.
"Gemma is a very good singer."

"Yes, she is. But Daniela, you are a good singer, *too*,"
says Jenny. "A very good singer." Jenny smiles at
Daniela.

"No, I'm not," Daniela says.

The next day, Gemma meets the band again.
"Hello, Gemma," says Tyler.
The band is happy with their new singer.
Everybody is very excited. Gemma is very excited, too.

Gemma gives some clothes to David and John.
"These clothes are for you," she says.
"But I don't want to wear these," David says. "I don't
like them."
Gemma says, "And we have a new name for the band.
It's on the clothes." It says 'Gemma and Hot Rock.'
"The band's name is 'Hot Rock', not 'Gemma and Hot
Rock!'" says Faye. "We don't want a new name."

Gemma says, "Let's sing some pop songs."
Faye says, "I don't want to play pop music."
"But I want to play pop music," says Gemma. "And I'm the singer."
John says, "But we are a rock band. We are not a pop band."
"And this band is *everybody's* band, not yours," says Faye.

The next day Faye, Tyler, David, and John see Daniela.
"Daniela, we want you to be in our band," Faye says. "We want you to sing with us!"
"Me?" says Daniela. "Really?" she says. "Can I be in your band? But, what about Gemma?" she asks.
Faye says, "Gemma doesn't sing for us now."
"Thank you, thank you, thank you," says Daniela.

Old Boat, New Boat

Written by
Rob Waring and **Maurice Jamall**

Before You Read

to clean

money

to fix something

truck

to paint

window

to sell

broken

beach

new boat

engine

old boat

In the story

Tyler

Faye

David

Ryan

Mr. Walsh

"Let's put it here," Mr. Walsh says to his son, Ryan.
Mr. Walsh has an old boat. He does not want it now.
They are putting his old boat on the beach.
Ryan says, "But, Dad, we can't put the boat here!"
Mr. Walsh says, "Ryan, it's okay. Nobody is looking."

Ryan helps his father. They put the old boat on the beach. Ryan sees a man. The man is walking his dog on the beach. "Dad," he says, "Somebody is coming. Come on! Let's go!" Ryan's father says, "Okay. Let's go."

The next morning, some people come to the beach.
One of the boys sees the old boat. His name is Tyler.
"Look at that!" says Tyler. "That's a nice boat!" he says.
Tyler's friend David says, "No, it's not. It's broken. It's no good."
Their friend Faye is looking at the boat, too.

Tyler says, "But we can fix it, and then we can have it!"
David says, "But it's not ours."
"I know. It's not ours," says Tyler. ". . . but nobody
wants it. We can fix it, and then it can be *our* boat."
"Tyler, that's a great idea," says Faye.

Then, two men come to the beach. They look at the boat.
"What are you doing?" David asks one man.
"We're taking the boat away," says the man.
David asks, "Whose boat is it?"
"I don't know," says the man. "It's a good boat, but nobody wants it."

"Can we have it?" asks Tyler. "We can fix the boat," he says.
"That's a great idea," says the man.
Tyler asks, "So, can we have it, please?"
The man says, "Yes, I think it's okay."
"Great! Thanks," Tyler says. He's very happy.

"Let's come back and get it on Saturday," says Faye. David says, "My father has a truck. He doesn't work on Saturday. He can help us."

"But the boat has no engine," says David. "And we don't have any money."

"I know!" says Faye. "But we can work and get some money. Then we can buy things for the boat."

"Good thinking!" says David.

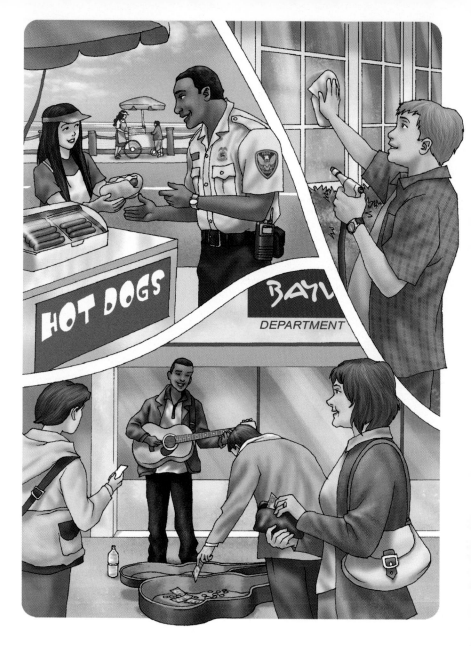

The next day they work to get some money.
Faye sells some hot dogs at the beach. Tyler plays music in the town. And David cleans windows. They get a lot of money. They can buy many things for the boat.

On Saturday, they take the boat to David's house. David's father, Mr. Robinson helps them. He gives them an engine for the boat.
Tyler and Mr. Robinson fix the boat.
Faye and David paint it. It is looking good now.
But Ryan is watching them.

Tyler says, "This old boat looks great now!"
"This *new* boat looks great, Tyler," says Faye.
Everybody smiles. They are very happy to have a boat.
"Let's take the boat to the beach," says David. "And let's go out in it."
Mr. Robinson takes the boat to the beach.

On the beach Ryan sees the boat.
"Wow, my boat looks great now," he thinks. He wants it back.
He says, "That's my boat! I want it back."
"No, Ryan," says Faye. "It's *our* boat."
Ryan says, "Give it back to me! It's mine."
"Do you really want your *old* boat, Ryan?" asks Tyler.
Ryan says, "Yes I do. Give me back my boat."

"Okay," says Tyler. "You can have it."

Tyler takes some things out of the boat. "But these are ours. You can't have them," he says.

They start taking things off the boat.

"Stop!" says Ryan. "That's my boat! Those things are mine!"

Faye says, "And this is our engine. Now give us money for the paint."

David says, "And give us money for fixing it."

The man comes back to the beach. He hears them talking.
"Is this your boat?" the man asks Ryan.
Ryan says, "Yes, it's mine."
"Oh, you put this boat on the beach. Then give me $200,"
says the man. "You can't put this on the beach."
Ryan is worried. "$200?" he thinks.
"Umm . . . no," he says now. "It's not my boat. It's theirs."

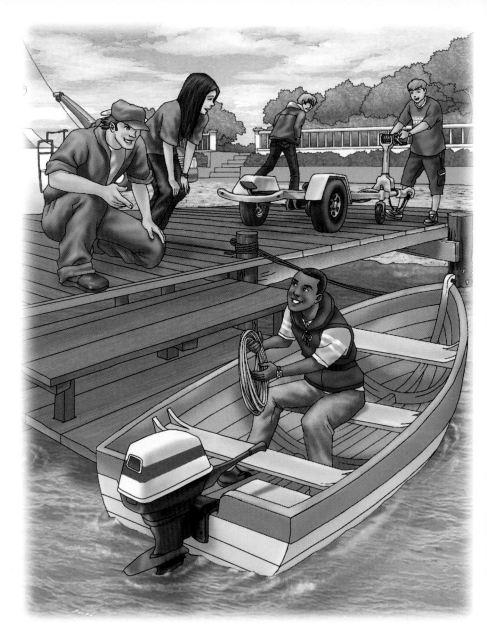

Ryan goes away. Tyler looks at the man. They smile.
"Thanks," says Tyler.
"You have a great new boat now," says the man.
David says, "Ryan's *old* boat. But our *new* boat!"

The Cave

Written by
Rob Waring and **Maurice Jamall**

Before You Read

to drive (a boat)		shark's teeth		
to open		water (the sea)		
to push		cold		
boat		dark		
cave		heavy		
key		interesting		
lamp		old	80 years old	
newspaper		wet		

In the story

Faye

John

Tyler

David

Daniela

"What a great day," says John to his friends.
John, Daniela, Tyler, and David are in their boat.
Faye is driving the boat. Faye is good at driving boats.
"Let's go over there!" says Faye. "It looks interesting."
"Okay, let's go," says everybody.

Tyler sees something. He shows it to his friends. "Look, what's that?" he asks.

"Let's go and look," says John. "Is that a cave?" he asks.

Tyler says, "Yes. Wow! Let's go in."

They drive the boat to the cave.

They go into the cave. It is very dark.
"John, can you see?" asks Faye.
John says, "No, it's too dark. I can't see."
Daniela is worried. She doesn't like the dark cave.
"It's very dark. I don't want to go in," says Daniela.
"It's okay, Daniela," says Tyler.

But soon they can see. They get out of the boat and look around the cave.
There are many interesting things in the cave.
There are some old books, lamps, and newspapers.
Faye sees something big.
"Wow!" says Faye. "Wow! Look at that!
What's that old thing?" she asks.
Tyler says, "I don't know.
But it's really interesting."

David sees something. "Hey, Daniela. What's this?" asks David.
He shows Daniela some shark's teeth.
Daniela says, "Stop that! David! Take it away!"
"Daniela, it's okay," says David.
"Why are these things in the cave?" asks John. "I think this is
somebody's cave. Somebody lives here."
"I don't think so," says Daniela. "These things are too old.
Nobody comes here now."

"Look at this newspaper," says Faye. "It's from 1979! It's really old!"
"Here are some more things. These are really interesting," says David. He shows Tyler some old things.
Tyler says, "This is a key. It looks really old. Why is it here?"
"I don't know," David says.

John sees an old bed. "Look at this old bed," John says. "It's great."

David shows Faye something. He asks, "What's this, Faye?"

"I don't know," she says. "But it's really great. I love this cave."

Daniela says, "But I don't like it. It's too dark in here. It's cold. Can we go?"

Daniela and David look at the boat and the water.
"Oh, no! Look!" says Daniela. "The water's coming in!"
"Let's get out," says David. He gets into the boat.
David and Daniela want to get out of the cave.
"We can't get out!" says David.

The water is high now. The boat cannot get out of the cave. David says, "We can't get out of the cave! What can we do?" "Oh no!" says Daniela again. "Where can we get out?" she asks.
"Daniela, it's okay," says Faye.
"Wait! It's okay. Don't worry, Daniela," says John. "The water doesn't come up to here. See? These things are not wet."

Tyler isn't worried. He looks around the cave.
Tyler sees something. He tells everyone. "Look!
We can get out of here. We can go this way."
"Great!" says Faye. "Let's go."
"You go first, John," says Faye.
"Next, Daniela can go, then David, Tyler, and me,"
she says.

Daniela and John get to the top.
John says, "Hey, everybody, there's a door! We can get out! But it looks heavy."
The door is too heavy and very old. He cannot open it. He pushes the door, but it does not open. "Oh, no! We can't get out," John says.
Everyone is worried now.

"I can't open it," says John. "I don't have the key."
"Oh no. I can help," says Daniela. She helps John.
They push the door.
"Push, Daniela," says John. But the door does not open.
David goes up to them. He has the old key.
"Daniela, is this the key?" David asks.

David gives the key to Daniela. She puts the key in the door.

"It's very heavy," says John. "Help me, Daniela."

"Let's push," she says. They push the door open.

"It's open!" says John. "We can get out."

"Come on, everybody," says Daniela. She is happy. She can get out now.

Everybody gets out of the cave. They are not worried now. "I like it here," says John. "This cave is great. Let's come back tomorrow and get the boat."
"You can. But not me!" says Daniela. "I'm not coming back!"
John smiles at Daniela. Daniela smiles back.